PRAISE FOR

Emotional Inheritance

"Beautiful, artistic, and elegant. Dr. Atlas skillfully uses stories from her practice to explore the archeology of transgenerational trauma. The descriptions of the therapeutic process pull you in; you come to know both patient and therapist. In doing so, you cannot help but reflect on your own journey. *Emotional Inheritance* is a gem for anyone, but it is an essential read for those seeking to understand trauma, therapy, and the healing process."

–Bruce D. Perry, MD, PhD, coauthor
(with Oprah Winfrey) of *What Happened to You?*

———

"Dr. Atlas writes with profound living compassion for those who have carried, in their bodies, minds, hearts, spirits, and souls, the most often unspoken and secret traumas of their own hurt elders. As a first-generation American child growing up in my tough family of war refugees, deportees—the ethnically cleansed, struggling immigrants, I humbly assert that I know about generational traumas in depth. I recognize Dr. Atlas as one who writes in full, knowing detail about what I call in my work 'the generational wound.'"

–Dr. Clarissa Pinkola Estés Reyés,
author of *Women Who Run with the Wolves*

———

"With elegance, Galit Atlas explains the troubling and nourishing aspects of our emotional inheritances. She deftly shows why the hurts and stuckness that can plague us can be faced and, yes, dissolved. Contemporary psychoanalysis at its best. And good storytelling too."

— Susie Orbach, author of *Fat Is a Feminist Issue*

"Galit Atlas has given us a gift with her book *Emotional Inheritance*. With warmth and compassion, she is able to show the reader the ways our present challenges could be linked to our inherited past. Using patient stories and her own experiences, we are taken on a journey of discovery. By sharing these stories, she gives us a glimpse behind our own curtains and helps us understand that if we are open to the possibility of hope, now might be the right time to break the silence our ancestors have held for so long."

— SHARON SALZBERG, author of *Real Happiness*

———

"Galit Atlas's *Emotional Inheritance* is insightful, perceptive, and provocative—but also tender, touching, and personal. Talented clinicians are not always talented writers, but Dr. Atlas is, and her stories will stay with you. The world of epigenetics is in its infancy for most of us, but Dr. Atlas uses ordinary language to explain how we are born with psychological legacies that we can not escape but which we can, with her help, understand."

— JULIET ROSENFELD, author of *The State of Disbelief*

———

"This book is full of great wisdom, expertise, and humanity. An important, terrific, gripping read."

— DR. ANNE ALVAREZ, author of *Live Company*

———

"A powerful, lucid, deeply empathic exploration of the legacy of generational trauma, *Emotional Inheritance* makes clear that Galit Atlas is not only a gifted psychoanalyst, but a gifted writer as well. I loved this book and was stirred by it."

— DANI SHAPIRO, author of *Inheritance*

"*Emotional Inheritance* offers extraordinary insight to readers who feel stuck in lifelong patterns and sense they are haunted by ghosts from their family's past. Dr. Atlas deftly shares her own history and those of her patients while seamlessly weaving in the relevant psychological research. Dr. Atlas's book reads like a propulsive page-turner while also offering deep psychological insights about inherited trauma and family secrets. This book will undoubtedly change lives and help readers unlock their unfulfilled potential."

— CHRISTIE TATE, author of *Group*

———

"A truly wise and daring book, *Emotional Inheritance* is an utterly compelling account of how the unconscious passage of trauma from one generation to the next is revealed in psychotherapy. With her special gift for evocative narrative, Dr. Atlas makes us present as witnesses to powerful stories of sorrows held in secret, of children who carry those sorrows forward, knowing without knowing what darkens their lives. Illuminating the meaning of such histories with splendid insights, this book will deeply satisfy whoever has wondered what psychoanalysis can offer in the present world."

— DR. JESSICA BENJAMIN, author of *The Bonds of Love*

———

"An intimate, textured, and compassionate exploration of intergenerational trauma, how it is carried and transmitted within families, and how it can be skillfully invited in, recognized, attenuated, and perhaps resolved through the therapeutic relationship, metabolizing what has hitherto not been named or nameable."

— JON KABAT-ZINN, author of
The Healing Power of Mindfulness

"Galit Atlas takes up Tolstoy's assertion—'Happy families are all alike; every unhappy family is unhappy in its own way'—as she narrates the ways in which traumas are uniquely held within families. Atlas tells the layered stories of her patients as their traumas reverberate with her own history of trauma and loss. The intimacy of the storytelling captures the recognition and repair that Atlas undertakes with her patients. Together they exhume the secrets and the ghosts that carry and bury trauma, pulling the reader into the present through the past, in order to break into the potential that is the future. Such potential is not a simple, sunny vale. Unhappy families are not made unthinkingly happy. But as Atlas demonstrates through her graceful generosity, bringing secrets and ghosts into the daylight offers the potential for new stories, more life, and the liberation called happiness."

— KEN CORBETT, PhD, author of *A Murder Over a Girl*

———

"An illuminating book. The stories Dr. Atlas shares reveal the potency of our inherited wounds, showing how the experiences of our ancestors shape our lives in quiet but far-reaching ways, and how we all have the potential to heal."

— LORI GOTTLIEB, author of *Maybe You Should Talk to Someone*

"A powerful, lucid, deeply empathic exploration
of the legacy of generational trauma. I loved this
book." —Dani Shapiro, author of *Inheritance*

Emotional
Inheritance

A THERAPIST,
HER PATIENTS, AND THE
LEGACY OF TRAUMA

Galit Atlas, PhD

THE
Emotional
Inheritance
WORKBOOK

DR. GALIT ATLAS

Bookswork Press

To those who choose to know

TABLE OF CONTENTS

What is Emotional Inheritance?

Every family carries some history of trauma. Every trauma is held within a family in a unique way and leaves its emotional mark on those who are yet to be born.

IN THE LAST DECADE, contemporary psychoanalysis and empirical research have expanded the literature on epigenetics and inherited trauma, investigating the ways in which trauma is transmitted from one generation to the next and held in our minds and bodies as our own. In studying the intergenerational transmission of trauma, clinicians investigate how our ancestors' trauma is passed down as an emotional inheritance, leaving a trace in our minds and in those of future generations. Emotional inheritance is about experiences that belong not only to us but to our parents, grandparents, and great-grandparents, and about the ways they impact our lives. It is these secrets that often keep us from living to our full potential. They affect our mental and physical health, create gaps between what we want for ourselves and what we are able to have, and haunt us like ghosts.

Our emotional inheritance not only involves the transmission of feelings but also the ways in which we learn to cope with and defend against pain and guilt. My book, *Emotional Inheritance*, focuses on the different ways our parents' and grandparents' histories, without our conscious awareness, impact our mental health, the choices we make and cannot make, and our well-being.

My hope is that reading the excerpts included here and journaling in response to the questions that follow will help you dive into and explore your own particular emotional inheritance and the way it impacts your life.

* * *

I was reminded of how powerful this kind of self-reflection can be at a workshop I led recently for a group of therapists. I open most workshops with the question: "Who in this room knows what their emotional inheritance is?" Usually, about half of the people raise their hands.

We discuss clinical cases and the stories in *Emotional Inheritance*, noticing the ways that trauma experienced by one generation can have a profound influence on subsequent ones.

At the end of these workshops, I ask people again, "Who can make a link between their family history and their own life, choices, and struggles?" We end up with almost every person in the room raising their hands.

In one of those workshops, a woman stood up at the end to tell us what she realized as she was reflecting on her family history. She shared with the group that her grandmother had died giving birth to her father and that in her previous career, she was a midwife—but until our discussion that day, she had never made a connection between the two things. It was the first time she realized that her choice to become a midwife was colored by the wish to save women in labor and was directly, yet unconsciously, related to her father's tragic history.

We should never underestimate the extent to which our emotional inheritance is held in ways that are unknown to us, even if they are hiding in plain sight.

HOW TO USE THIS BOOK

Welcome to this work, the work of understanding yourself, which is nothing less than the work of being fully alive!

Many readers of my book, *Emotional Inheritance: A Therapist, Her Patients, and the Legacy of Trauma*, have asked, "How do I move forward? Where do I go from here?" While of course no book can replace professional therapeutic work, this workbook is designed to help you think about the ties connecting the past, present, and future of your own life.

Unpacking your emotional inheritance is a profound process. If you are reading this, it is because you've made the courageous decision to open that door and rather than turn away from the hurt of the past, to walk toward it. You have made the decision to become an active agent in owning your life.

I invite you on a journey; a journey that will open a space in which to think, to feel, to dream, and to generate insight and growth.

There is no right or wrong way to do this workbook. The goal is to open up a realm for reflection and awareness; to connect the dots, to put the unspeakable into words, and to allow yourself the freedom to invite in new ideas and emotional possibilities.

Please take the time to journal, free-associate and welcome any thoughts and feelings that come up when you write your answers.

Pay special attention to what you don't know, to the information that is missing, and to any other gaps that you find in your family narratives.

If you find yourself judging your thoughts or feelings, make a note of this in your journal. It will be beneficial to then go back and reflect on the specific questions or answers that triggered judgment or guilt.

After you start your journey, you should expect to have more dreams at night. Try to write your dreams in your journal, as well as any daydreams and thoughts that you have throughout the day. You can use the last pages to write your thoughts, feelings and dreams.

You can go back and add material to questions you've already answered.

As you move forward, please hear my voice asking you to slow down, to allow yourself to not know, to breathe, and to forgive yourself.

* * *

PART ONE

Your Life

DRAW A "GENOGRAM" of your life.

Use a pencil to do this exercise.

Draw a circle on the paper that represents yourself. Your circle can be in any size and you can place it anywhere on the paper. Write your name, or "ME," in or outside of it.

Now draw a circle for people who are close to or as distant from you or who have or had an impact (positive or negative) on your life. You can place their circles as close or as distant to yourself as you experience them. You can include people in or outside of your family, people who are an active part of your life or not, people who are alive or who have passed away (use a broken line to represent dead people), pets, or anyone else that is meaningful to you. Write their name in or outside of the circle.

Please know that this genogram is a map that reflects only your current state, and it will change over time.

Here is an example of a genogram:

My genogram:

Look at your genogram. Write down the answers. What do you feel when you are looking at this genogram?

What is the thing that appears most obvious to you?

What, if anything, troubles you about this picture of your life?

If relevant, what specifically makes you feel good about this picture of your life?

How big or small are you in relation to other family members?

Who is in the biggest circle?

Who is in the smallest one?

How many members of your family are in this picture?

Who is left out? Why do you think they are left out?

Is there anyone in this picture from whom you are estranged, or with whom you have an unresolved issue?

| Who are the people you are the closest to in this picture?

| Does any circle merge with or touch yours?

Who is further away from you in this picture?

Can you recognize groups and coalitions in this picture?

Is there anyone in this picture with whom you have an unhealthy relationship?

Journal what this exercise meant to you. What did it stir up? What did it confirm? What did you learn about yourself? Write down any feelings that you are left with.

Fill the boxes.

Who in your family did you
want to be like?

Who in your family were you
afraid to be like?

Who in your family do you
find yourself most similar to?

Who in your family do you
find yourself the opposite of?

As you read through the list below

- Put a star next to any feelings, symptoms, and diagnoses that you have from a professional or self-diagnosis.

- Mark any feelings, symptoms, and diagnoses that your family members have or "should" have.

- Indicate F=Father, M=Mother S- Sister B= Brother GF= Grandfather, etc…

Anxiety

Depression

Impulsivity

Stress

Bipolarity

Paranoia

Eating disorder

Psychosis

Dissociation

Illness anxiety

Addiction

Unpredictable moods

OCD (Obsessive Compulsive Disorder)

Phobia

Autism

Nightmares or night terrors

Anger

Sadness

Jealousy

Disappointment

Shame or Embarrassment

People pleaser

Judgmental

Proud

Resentful

Oppositional

Shut down

Dishonest

Manipulative

Perfectionist

Better than others/superior

Not as good as others/inferior

Extremist

PART TWO

The Parents
of Your Parents

*We inherit family traumas
we weren't told about.*

WE ALL HAVE OUR PHANTOMS. But as the psychoanalysts Maria Torok and Nicolas Abraham once wrote, 'What haunts are not the dead, but the gaps left within us by the secrets of others.' They were referring to intergenerational secrets and unprocessed experiences that very often don't have a voice or an image associated with them but loom in our minds nonetheless. We carry emotional material that belongs to our parents and grandparents, retaining losses of theirs that they never fully articulated. We feel these traumas even if we don't consciously know them. Old family secrets live inside us.

When we think about our grandparents, we tend to have limited knowledge. Since they are two generations apart from us, we know certain things about them, but not others. We may have strong memories of them, but these memories are sometimes imagined or idealized.

This section is an invitation to dig a little deeper. It might involve doing some detective work, an approach that is a close cousin of psychoanalysis. Sigmund Freud himself was a big fan of Sherlock Holmes, and in some ways, what we are doing here borrows Holmes's methods: gathering evidence, searching for truths beneath the surface, and seeking out hidden realities.

Please dedicate a separate space to each of your parents' parents.

Did you know your parents' parents (your grandparents)? If not, why not? If you did, what are/ were they like? Use three words to describe each of your grandparents.

Are they still alive? If not, when did they die?

How did their death impact your parent?

How did their death impact you?

When you think about each of your grandparents, what is one story about them or memory that comes to mind?

Describe each of your grandparents' history. What was their childhood like? Did they have any traumas? Think about personal, racial, and social traumas. Here are some examples of experiences that can be traumatic: immigration; racism; war; genocide; poverty; early losses; suicide; illness; accidents; miscarriage; abortion; divorce; sexual, verbal, or physical abuse; neglect, or abandonment.

Describe grandparent #1's childhood.

Describe grandparent #2's childhood.

Describe grandparent #3's childhood.

Describe grandparent #4's childhood.

Add any other person who is like a parent to one of your parents and/or a grandparent to you.

Reflect on the positive or negative role of traditions, rituals, and family customs in your relationship with your grandparents and these figures. Consider any racial, cultural, political, or societal influences that were significant during your grandparents' upbringing. How have these influences been passed down to you, shaping your emotional outlook and values?

Consider the positive and negative values and beliefs that were important to your grandparents. Which of these values do you still hold onto, or act against, and how do they influence your own emotional attitudes and behaviors?

What kind of relationship did your grandparents have with your parent(s)? Please describe each of your parents' relationship with each of their parents.

Did any of your grandparents have secrets that you now know about? While many family secrets involve money or sex, it's not unusual that traumatic experiences are kept as secrets. Please reflect on any secrets that you are aware of.

What subjects were avoided in each of your parents' families?
What were you not allowed to talk about? This is a hard question, since many times we are so used to our family dynamic that we don't know what is missing. Here we should try to follow the omission. Please write separately about each of your parents' families.

What don't you know? Are there gaps in what you know about them? If so, try to notice what is missing.

Is there one grandparent your parent (their child) identified with most strongly? Or one your parent had the most trouble connecting to, or is estranged from?

Is there one grandparent with whom you identify most strongly? Or one you had the most trouble connecting to?

EXERCISE

Think about each of your grandparents. If that person isn't alive, or if that person were to die today, what is the one thing you regret or would regret not having asked them? What is the one thing you regret or would regret not having told them?

Use the space below to journal and reflect on the link between your grandparents and your emotional inheritance. What did this section stir up? What did it confirm? What did you learn about yourself? Write down any feelings, associations, or thoughts that you are left with.

PART THREE

Your Parents and the People Who Raised You

*As children we are tuned in to
our attachment figures, to the people we
are dependent on. We register not only
what they say, but also, and especially,
what they don't say.*

OUR EMOTIONAL INHERITANCE shapes our behaviors, our perceptions, our feelings, and even our memories. From a young age, we learn to follow our parents' signals; we learn to walk around their wounds, try not to mention and absolutely not touch what mustn't be disturbed. In our attempt to avoid their pain and our own, we blind ourselves to that which is right before our eyes.

This section on your parents applies to the people who raised you, whether they are your biological parents, adopted or foster parents, or other family members.

From birth, the world of our parents is the only world we know, and we are affected by them in profound ways for which we have no perspective. The work in this section is to try to examine that relationship as if you were seeing your own life—and your parents' lives—for the first time.

Trauma is often communicated between parents and children in two different pathways. I would call those the "too-muchness" and "the not-enoughness."

In some families, there is "too muchness"—excessive story-telling with too many details (as in Chapter One of *Emotional Inheritance*) which floods and dysregulates the next generation, and often generates intense feelings of guilt. That is also the case in families where there is abuse, and when one generation inflicts their own pain on the other (as in Chapters Two and Ten of *Emotional Inheritance*).

In other families, there is a void—"not-enoughness"—where the family is haunted by secrets and by the "ghosts of the unspeakable"; what we are not allowed to know, to speak, or to think about (as in Chapters Three, Four and Five of *Emotional Inheritance*).

This next section will help you understand your family style and how it has impacted your life.

It will focus on family patterns and repetitions, unconscious identifications with the previous generation, as well as the wish to heal your parents and repair past wounds.

Who were the people who raised you?
Think of three words that describe each of them:

Parent 1:

Parent 2:

Add any other person who raised you.

Think of three words to describe your childhood relationship with each of your parents:

Parent 1:

Parent 2:

Add any other person who raised you.

Think of three words to describe your current relationship with each of your parents:

Parent 1:

Parent 2:

Add any other person who raised you.

Which quality of each of your parents triggered you most?

Which quality of each of your parents did you like or appreciate most?

Did you lose either of your parents to death at a young age? If so, how do you think it impacted you then and now?

If your parents are alive, has your relationship with each of them changed? If so, in what ways?

Did you have stepparents? What was your relationship with them? How did they impact your life?

Were there any other adults who took care of you or with whom you were close? Who were they? What role did they play in your life?

Reflect on your earliest memories of emotional interactions with your parents. How did their emotions—or lack of them—influence your own at that time?

What were each of their parenting styles? Were they very strict, or more permissive?

Were they distant from you? In what ways?

Were they judgmental of you? In what ways?

Were you afraid of either of your parents? Why?

Did either of your parents ever hurt you? In what ways?

Did either of your parents leave you when you were a child, whether it was their choice or not?

Reflect on the concept of emotional boundaries within your family. What was each of your parents' relationships with boundaries? Did you experience a lack of boundaries?

Is there a parent with whom you identified most strongly?

Is there a parent with whom you had the most trouble connecting, or from whom you are estranged?

If your parents were together, what was their relationship to each other?

If they were separated, what do you know about their separation?

Did you take a side or prefer one of them? Did you live with only one of them?

Please describe in detail what you know about your parents' early lives. What were their childhoods like? Do you think of your parents' childhoods as traumatic? As good? As bad? Did they have any traumatic events in their childhood?

What do you think about the way each of your parents describes their childhood? Do you think they tend to minimize or exaggerate their experiences?

Do you think of either of your parents as strong?

Do you think of either of your parents as weak?

Do you think of either of your parents as broken?

Do you think of either of your parents as inspiring?

What don't you know about your parents? Are there gaps in what you know about them? If so, try to notice what is missing.

For each of your parents: describe in detail one of their childhood memories. Please note how old they were when it took place, and where it happened. Share any details that you know.

What is your feeling about that memory? Does it make you sad, happy, angry, distressed, apathetic, or any other feeling?

In what way does the memory you describe reflect their overall childhood?

What were your parents's relationships with their siblings?

Did either of your parents lose a sibling at a young age, or have a sibling who struggled in life? Think about that legacy in your family.

Did anything traumatic happen to either of your parents when you were young? If so, describe:

Did either of your parents experience loss when you were young?

When you were young, were either of your parents sick or struggling, either emotionally or physically? Please describe.

Did you have a wish to help or heal them?

Did you have a wish to be away from them?

| Did you ever wish you had different parents?

| Did you ever struggle in similar ways? If so, describe:

TOO-MUCHNESS OR NOT-ENOUGHNESS

What is your family's style of communication? Write down the way each of your parents talked about the past.

Did your parents want to or insist on telling you stories from their childhood? If so, did they tell you detailed stories?

Were their stories ever inappropriate or scary?

Did they tell you things that you didn't want to know?

Do you remember your emotional or physical reaction to their stories?

What details don't you know about each of your parents' history? What subjects were avoided in the house where you grew up, things you were not allowed to talk about?

Did either of your parents have secrets that you now know about?
If so, describe.

If there is a secret that you now know, when did you find out?

What was your reaction?

Do your parents know that you know?

How did that secret impact you?

If one of your parents or important caregivers were to die today, what is the one thing you would regret not having asked them about? What is the one thing you would regret not having told them?

Use these pages to free-associate in response to these questions.

In what form did your family history transmit to you (too-muchness, not-enoughness, both?) How did it impact you? Did you find that you identify with one of your parents and with their pain, try to help and heal them, or feel guilty for not doing so? Did you find that you try to disconnect from your parents' pain? Did you try to push them away?

Write an imaginary letter to one of your parents. Express your feelings, insights, and needs about the past, present, or future. Share anything you have learned about your family so far. Ask them for something that you need from them. Make a request even if you think they will not be able to give it to you, or that it will hurt them.

PART FOUR

Your Childhood

AS CHILDREN, WE EXPERIENCE our parents' fears and inherit them, perceiving the world the way our parents did, defending ourselves in similar ways. We are invested in keeping our family secrets but mostly we are trying to keep secrets from ourselves. What we can't let ourselves know leaves us unfamiliar to ourselves, unable to know others or to be fully known by them. The growing ability to integrate and process pain helps us find meaning, heal, live life to the fullest, and raise the next generation with honesty and integrity.

Did you feel loved?

Did you feel smart?

Did you feel lonely?

Did you feel understood?

Did you often feel humiliated?

Did your family support you?

Did you ever feel ashamed of your parents, siblings or other family members?

Did you feel safe as a child at home or in the environment in which you grew up?

Did your family live in one place when you were a child, or did you move a lot?

Use three words to describe the kind of a child you were.

Who were you closest to?

Who took care of you when you were sick?

Was there trauma in your childhood? Describe your experience, if you can.

Did anyone else in your family suffer from similar trauma?

What is your first memory?

What is your happiest childhood memory? (That memory can be from any age, and include anything that made you happy.)

What is your most painful childhood memory?

What is your scariest childhood memory? That memory can include anything that was frightening at the time.

Did you lose anyone close, a friend, family member or a pet, when you were a child? If so, do you remember how you reacted? What impact did it have on who you are as an adult?

Do you have siblings? If so, what was your childhood relationship with them?

Did any of your siblings struggle in childhood? If so, how did it impact your family? How did your parents react? What was your feeling about that sibling?

Do you have any half brothers/half sisters or stepbrothers/stepsisters? If so, what was your childhood relationship with them?

What is your relationship with your stepsiblings today?

Was there a "favorite child" in your family? Describe in detail.

Write a letter to your childhood self. Include in your letter something that you know now but your childhood self couldn't know. Include in your letter anything you know or understand about the struggles of your childhood self. Include in your letter anything good that you now see in your childhood self.

PART FIVE

Finding Truth: Where Our Emotional Inheritance Hides

THE ABILITY TO LOVE, to invest in life, to create and fulfill our dreams, is in ongoing dialogue with our capacity to search for emotional truths, to tolerate pain, and to mourn. While our journeys to healing vary, each starts with the decision to search, to open the door, and, rather than turn away from the hurt of the past, to walk toward it. We choose to unpack our emotional inheritance, to be active agents in transforming our fate into destiny. The secrets of others become our own enigmas, and our secrets will inevitably find shelter and hide in the minds of others. The more concealed these secrets are, the more we become strangers to ourselves, held in captivity, afraid of the freedom to know and be known. The ghosts of the past are alive in our unconscious. To some degree, we are all gatekeepers of the unspeakable.

The truth can be elusive, and there can be more than one truth. We often spend our lives invested in—and dependent on—a narrative about our families, and about ourselves, that is constructed. Finding truths can be especially difficult if we cling to one narrative, and if we are afraid of knowing anything that would threaten it. But just as genetic testing can reveal hidden siblings or parentage, asking family members and the people who know them for more information can lead to a clearer understanding of hidden motivations and patterns in our lives.

When we ask, we might not get answers, or we might get confusing facts; this is all important information, as we are listening not only to what is said or done but also, and sometimes especially, to the gaps, the omissions, to what is not said.

Let's start with a little detective work.

Do you want to know more about your childhood, your parents, and their parents? Are you afraid of the answers? If so, who are you most afraid to talk to? What are you most afraid to find out?

Have you ever researched your family members? If so, what did you find?

Have you looked through your parents' old letters, photographs, or other memorabilia? If so, describe your experience.

Have you ever checked your genetic history? Has anyone else in your family ever done this? If so, describe anything you found out.

Have you ever asked uncomfortable questions? If so, did you get answers and what were the answers?

Have you ever recorded family members for an oral history of your family? If so, what was your experience like?

Choose one family member and ask them a question to which you are not too afraid to know the answer. Write down your experience.

NAMES

Names are a significant part of one's identity. In first sessions, I usually ask people about the meaning of their names, inquire who chose the names for them and why, and wonder if there are specific meanings or stories associated with their names. Names are connected to emotions, the hopes parents have for their child, who they think the child will become or want the child to become. A name reflects the parents' feelings about having that child. It contains remembrances from the past as well as a vision of the future.

Babies are often named after relatives or others who passed away. A child might be given the name of a person the parents loved, admired, or attributed certain characteristics to. The child's name might reflect certain expectations, responsibilities, or roles. For example, one of my patients was named after his mother's father, who died just before my patient was born. In therapy, we connected his name to the role he was assigned at birth, as his mother's caretaker. His mother described him as a mature and responsible baby, wise from a young age, whom she turned to for advice. Another patient was given a name by his mother that meant "mine." It turned out that his father was ambivalent about having a child; she felt this baby was hers alone. There is a profound meaning in naming a baby after a person who died in tragic circumstances, for example, a child or a person who died by suicide or was murdered. Doing so is often an expression of a wish not only to revive what was lost but also to repair the past and heal trauma.

What is the story behind your name? Write down your "name-story" and any details you know about it or imagine.

Were you named after a relative? What do you know about this relative?

What is the meaning of your name? For example, Maria can be translated to either mean "of the sea," "bitter," "beloved," or "rebellious." Did your name express hope, fear, or any other feeling?

How was your name chosen? Who chose it and why?

Write as many details as you know about your name and the connections you make between the choice of your name and your family dynamic and history.

BIRTH STORY

What is your birth story? Write any details you can put together about your birth story: What emotions or thoughts stand out the most in the stories about the time before you were born? Was your mother's pregnancy expected? Wanted? Do you know the actual story of your birth? If so, who was there, what was the environment into which you were born?

Write down any stories that your parents tell about your birth or anything that you feel is missing from that story.

In what way has the story of your birth shaped your understanding of your own journey and existence?

UNCONSCIOUS IDENTIFICATIONS
AND THE WISH TO REPAIR

Our emotional inheritance often comes from the parent we identify with or from the parent we wish we could save.

Are you aware of coalitions or subgroups in your family? If so, which group do you belong to?

When there is a conflict in your family, whose side are you usually on?

Who in your family do you think makes good decisions?

Is there anyone in your family who you feel has made sacrifices for you?

Is there anyone in your family you wish you were more similar to?

Is there anyone in your family whom you are afraid you are too much like?

Is there anyone in your family you believe was treated badly by another family member?

Is there anyone in your family whom you wish you could help or save?

Is there anyone in your family you feel has had bad luck?

Is there anyone in your family who didn't get enough recognition or appreciation?

Whom did you protect as a child?

Is there anyone in your family who you think needed protection that they didn't get?

Is your path in life similar to anyone else's in your family? You can include any personal or professional details.

Does your personal or professional path differ significantly from that of anyone else in your family?

Is there anyone in your family to whom you are most loyal?

Are you aware of any life choices you have made that were related to a family member's struggle, or experience? Your choice could be a form of repeating their experience, avoiding it, trying to do it better, or trying to fix it.

SURVIVOR GUILT

Survivor guilt is a feeling that is passed down from generation to generation. Survivors of trauma are left with an overwhelming amount of guilt and the next generation's experience is colored by that guilt. Survivor guilt is often unconscious and, therefore, hard to recognize.

Can you think about the survivors in your family and imagine what kind of guilt they might carry, why, and in relation to whom?

POTENTIAL SYMPTOMS OF SURVIVOR GUILT IN SECOND AND THIRD GENERATIONS

- Minimizing your own struggles or life experiences and comparing them to others, especially to your parents' or grandparents' trauma.

- A constant feeling that you have to be grateful and thankful for what you have.

- Difficulty in feeling happy and satisfied.

- Feelings of emptiness.

- Anxiety when good things happen.

- Difficulty separating from your parents.

- Feeling bad that you have more than other people have.

- Intense need to give your parents what you have and to take care of them.

Think about your potential inherited guilt. How many of those symptoms do you have? Use the space below to describe your experience.

PART SIX

Moving Beyond the Legacy of Trauma

THE SCARS OF OUR INHERITED trauma take their own unique shape. Our awareness, like detective work, follows the traces those ghosts leave in our minds. This awareness slowly sheds light on the ways the past affects and controls our present being. In ways that often feel mysterious, emotional material left unprocessed tends to appear and reappear in our lives. The unexamined life repeats itself and reverberates through the generations. The untold stories clamor for reenactment—they insist on being told. That which cannot be consciously identified forces itself into our reality and repeats itself. It is those now-seen patterns that we search for and unpack. Again and again, the human unconscious brings us to the original site of where things went wrong with the wish to do it all over again, repair the damage, and heal those who were hurt and wounded. We identify with previous generations—with those who have been injured, who have been humiliated, and who have died. In our fantasy, their cure is also our own. We plead for liberation from our bonds to the painful past and from the guilt of living and having a better life than the people who came before us.

As you have questioned your own narrative, examined your upbringing, and learned more about the hidden pasts of your parents—and their parents—you may have discovered new things about your family history and yourself. Such discoveries can be unsettling since they rearrange and often challenge the familiar ways we used to think about our lives. But these same discoveries might offer clues to your patterns and tendencies, your own reactivity, your vulnerability, and your life decisions. If you are just beginning this process, I applaud your courage.

How is your physical or mental health? Is there anything you wish you could change?

How is your work life? Is there anything you wish you could change?

How are your romantic relationships? Is there anything you wish you could change?

How are your family relationships? Are there any you wish you could change?

How are your friendships? Are there any you wish you could change?

Which of your relationships would you like to make closer in some way? Which of them would you wish to improve or repair?

Which of these relationships do you feel no longer serves you in a positive way?

Picture each of the important people in your life. If they were to die today, is there one thing you wish you had asked them while they were still alive? Is there one thing you wish you had told that person?

Draw a genogram of your *future* life. Use a pencil to do this exercise. Once again, draw a circle on the paper that represents yourself. Choose a size and location for your circle and write your name in or outside of it. Locate your significant relationships as close or as distant to yourself as you would like them. Please include every person in and outside of your family with whom you hope to have a meaningful relationship. Write their name in or outside of the circle.

Look at your genogram. How do you feel about this future picture of your relationships?

What is the thing that appears most different than in your previous genogram?

What makes you feel good in this picture?

Is there anything that makes you feel sad about this picture?

How many members of your family are in this picture? Who is left out?

Who did you leave out who was in the previous picture and who did you add?

Who are the people who are the closest to you here?

From whom are you disconnected?

Can you recognize groups and coalitions in this picture?

Is there any relationship resolution that occurs in this version?

Write a letter to your future self. Include anything that you learned about yourself or your family, anything that you became aware of, anything you are grateful for, and any wishes and hopes that you have for the future.

REFLECTION

Use the space below to journal and reflect on your emotional inheritance. Write down any new knowledge, feelings, insights, or thoughts that you are left with. Note anything you still wish to know, want to explore, or need to process.

To those who choose to know

You have now started your journey. You have opened a door.

Change doesn't happen in one day. But those who choose to know turn on a light that only gets brighter over time.

Keep reflecting, keep dreaming, keep writing down everything that comes to mind. In the next few months, new thoughts and feelings will continue to emerge. Links between past, present, and future might become lucid.

Come back to this workbook in a year, create a new genogram of your life, and compare it to the one from the previous year. Let me know what happened.

Galit Atlas

RESOURCES

If you need immediate help call 911 or visit your nearest emergency room.

Crisis text line
https://www.crisistextline.org/

National domestic violence hotline
800-799-7233

National sexual assault hotline
800-656-4673

American Psychological Association (APA)
https://www.apa.org/

National Institute for the Psychotherapies (NIP)
https://niptherapy.org/

NYU Postdoctoral Program for Psychotherapy and Psychoanalysis—Clinic Services
https://as.nyu.edu/departments/postdocpsychoanalytic/clinical-services.html

Psychology Today—therapy directory
https://www.psychologytoday.com/us/therapists

ABOUT THE AUTHOR

Dr. Galit Atlas is a renowned psychoanalyst and a faculty member of the New York University Postdoctoral Program in Psychotherapy & Psychoanalysis. She is the author of the international bestseller *Emotional Inheritance: A Therapist, Her Patients, and the Legacy of Trauma* (translated into 26 languages), as well as three books for clinicians and numerous articles. Atlas has been a contributor to the *New York Times*, the *Wall Street Journal*, the *LA Times* and more. A leader in the field of relational psychoanalysis, Dr. Atlas is a recipient of the André François Award, the Gradiva Award and the NADTA Research Award. Atlas teaches and lectures throughout the United States and internationally.

SPECIAL OFFER!

Share a video of your experience of *The Emotional Inheritance Workbook* on TikTok or Instagram. Send your video to info@booksworkpress.com and get a free ebook version of the workbook.

THOUGHTS, FEELINGS, DREAMS

THOUGHTS, FEELINGS, DREAMS

THOUGHTS, FEELINGS, DREAMS